HAL•LEONARD

ro Vocal®
BETTER THAN KARAOKE!

Grease

ISBN 13: 978-1-4234-4683-5

HAL•LEONARD®
CORPORATION
7777 W. BLUEMOUND RD. P.O. BOX 13819 MILWAUKEE, WI 53213

Visit Hal Leonard Online at
www.halleonard.com

CONTENTS

Freddy, My Love

Lyric and Music by Warren Casey and Jim Jacobs

Intro
Moderately

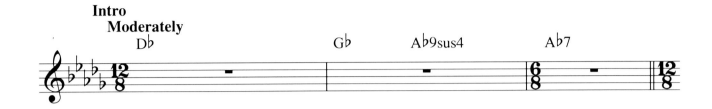

Verse

1. Fred - dy, my love, I miss you more than words can say.

Fred - dy, my love, please keep in touch while you're a - way.

Hear - ing from you can make the day ___ so much bet - ter, ___

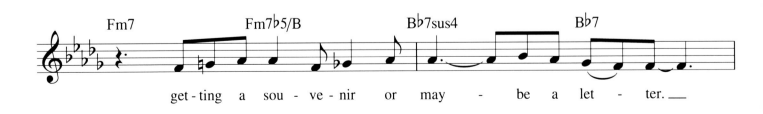

get - ting a sou - ve - nir or may - be a let - ter. ___

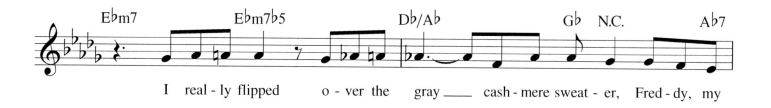

I real-ly flipped o-ver the gray ___ cash-mere sweat-er, Fred-dy, my

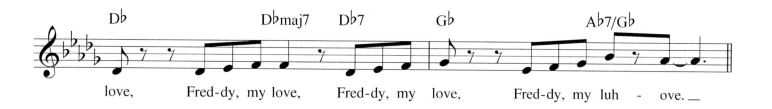

love, Fred-dy, my love, Fred-dy, my love, Fred-dy, my luh - ove. ___

Verse

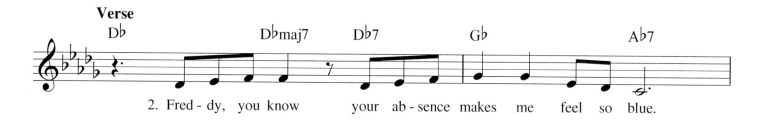

2. Fred - dy, you know your ab - sence makes me feel so blue.

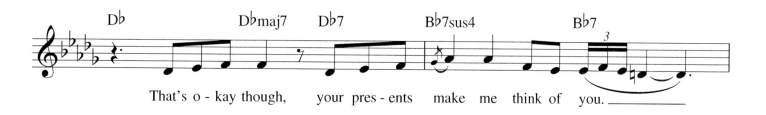

That's o - kay though, your pres - ents make me think of you. ___

My ma will have a heart at - tack ___ when she catch - es ___

those ped - al push - ers with the black ___ leath - er patch - es. ___

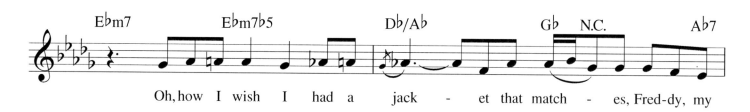

Oh, how I wish I had a jack - et that match - es, Fred-dy, my

love, Fred - dy, my love, Fred - dy, my love, Fred - dy, my luh - ove. __ Don't

Bridge

keep __ your let - ters from me, I thrill __ to ev - 'ry line. Your

spell - ing's kind - a crum - my, but hon - ey, so is mine. I

treas - ure ev - 'ry gift - y. The ring is real - ly nif - ty. You

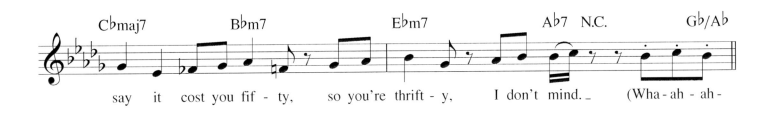

say it cost you fif - ty, so you're thrift - y, I don't mind. __ (Wha - ah - ah -

Verse

oh.) 3. Fred - dy, you'll see, you'll hold me in your arms some - day,

and I will be wear - ing your lac - ey lin - ge - rie.

Think-ing a - bout _ it, ___ my heart's pound - ing al-read - y, ___

know-ing when you come home we're bound ___ to go stead - y ___

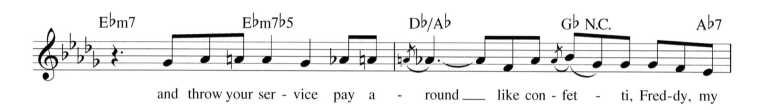

and throw your ser - vice pay a - round ___ like con - fet - ti, Fred-dy, my

love, Fred-dy, my love Fred-dy, my love, Fred-dy, my luh - ove. __

Fred-dy, my love, Fred-dy, my love, Fred-dy, my luh - ove. __

Fred - dy, my love.

Hopelessly Devoted to You

Words and Music by John Farrar

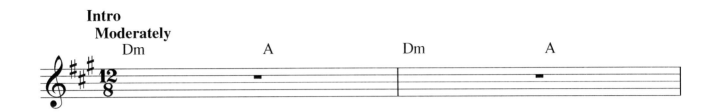

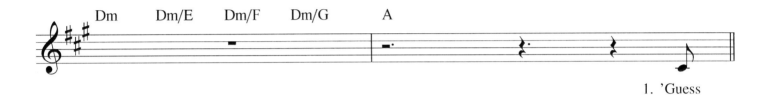

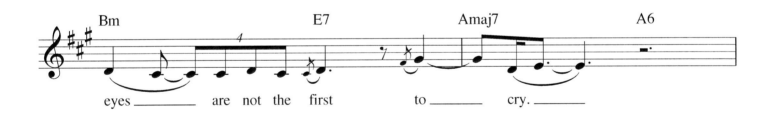

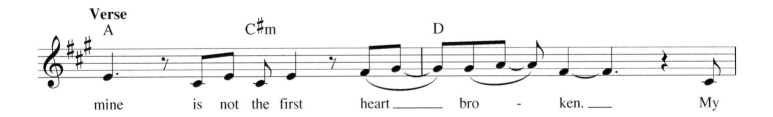

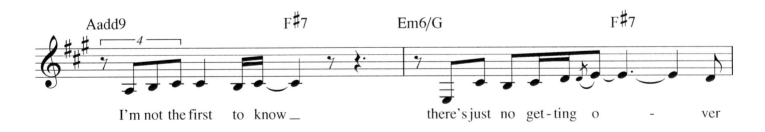

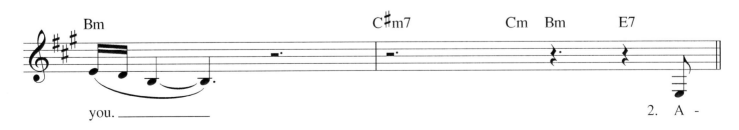

to ___ you, _____ hope - less - ly de - vot - ed ___

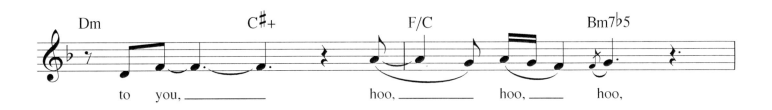

to you, _____ hoo, _____ hoo, _____ hoo,

hope - less - ly de - vot - ed _____ to you. _____

Verse

___ 3. My head is say - in', "fool, _____

___ for - get him." _____ My heart is say - in', "don't let him ___

___ go." _____ Hold on 'til the end,

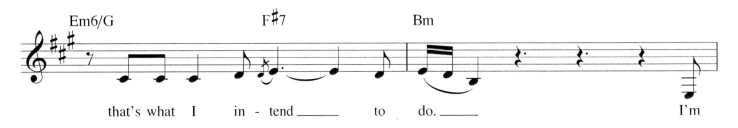

that's what I in - tend _____ to do. _____ I'm

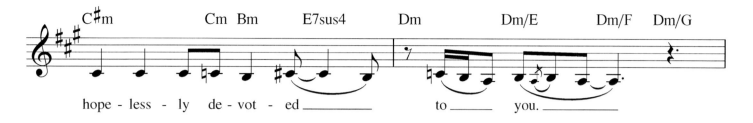

hope - less - ly   de - vot - ed _____   to _____   you. _____

Bridge

But   now   there's   no - where to hide   since you

pushed   my   love   a - side. __   I'm __   out   of   my   head, __

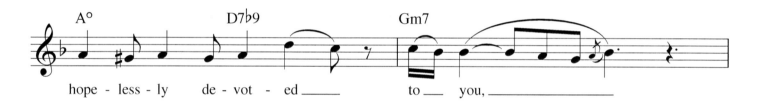

hope - less - ly   de - vot - ed _____   to __ you, _____

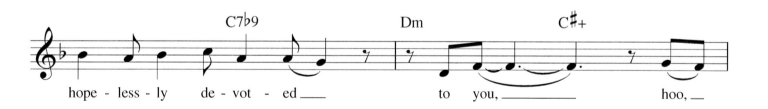

hope - less - ly   de - vot - ed ___   to   you, _____   hoo, __

hoo,   hoo, _____ hoo.   Hope - less - ly   de - vot - ed ___

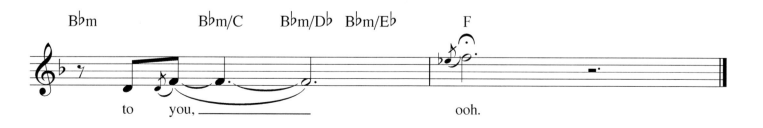

to   you, _____   ooh.

It's Raining on Prom Night

Lyric and Music by Warren Casey and Jim Jacobs

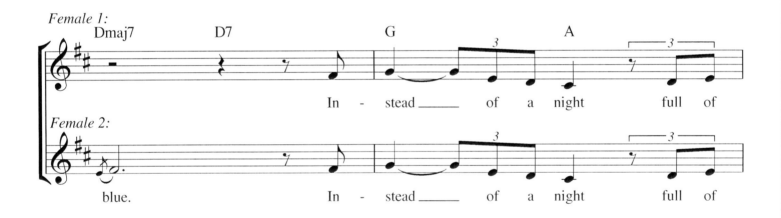

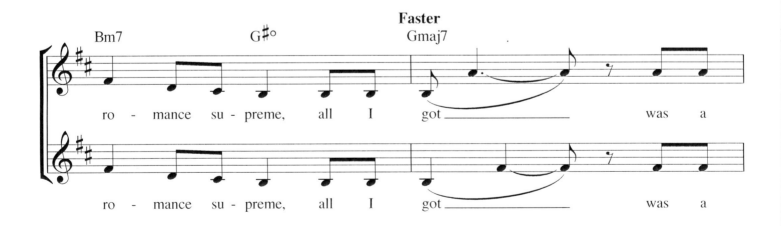

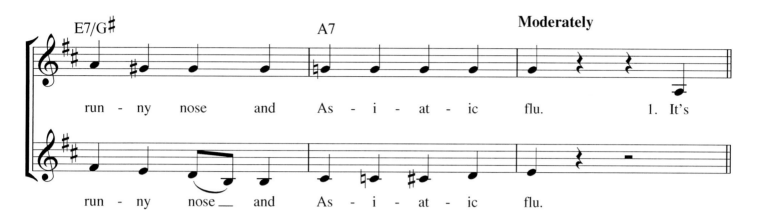

run - ny nose and As - i - at - ic flu. 1. It's

run - ny nose __ and As - i - at - ic flu.

Verse

rain - ing on prom night. My hair __ is a

It's rain - ing on __ prom night. Oh, __ my

mess. __ It's run - ning all o - ver my

hair is a mess. It's run - ning all o - ver,

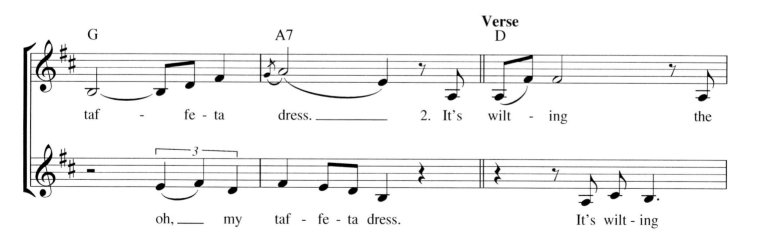

Verse

taf - fe - ta dress. ____ 2. It's wilt - ing the

oh, __ my taf - fe - ta dress. It's wilt - ing

Bm7 / G / A7

quilt - ing   in ___ my ___ Maid - en - form, _____ and mas-

the quilt - ing,   oh, ___ in   my   Maid - en - form.

D / Bm7 / G

car - a flows   right down my nose, _ be - cause ___ of the

Mas - car - a   flows   right down my   nose, ___ be - cause it's

Bridge

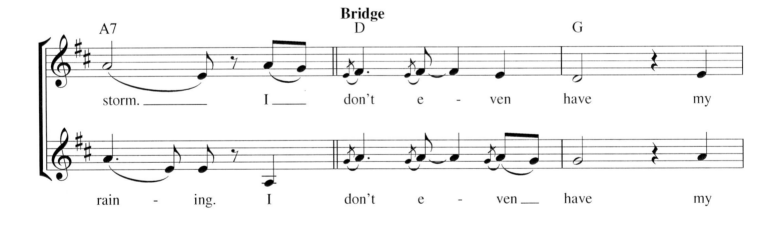

A7 / D / G

storm. ___ I ___ don't   e - ven   have   my

rain - ing. I   don't   e - ven ___ have   my

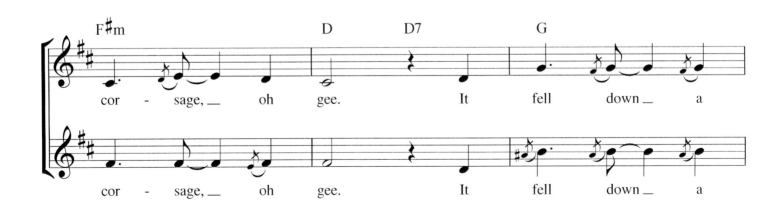

F#m / D   D7 / G

cor - sage, ___ oh gee.   It   fell   down ___ a

cor - sage, ___ oh gee.   It   fell   down ___ a

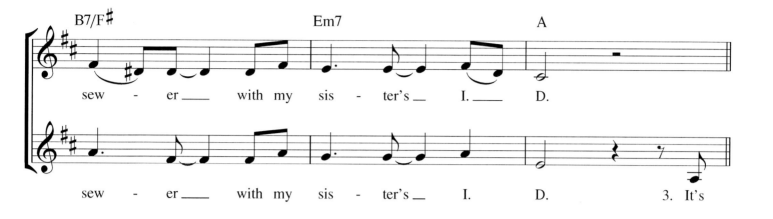

sew - er ___ with my sis - ter's ___ I. ___ D.

sew - er ___ with my sis - ter's ___ I. D. 3. It's

Verse

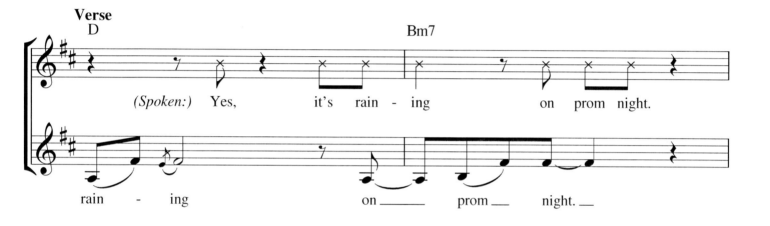

(Spoken:) Yes, it's rain - ing on prom night.

rain - ing on ___ prom ___ night. ___

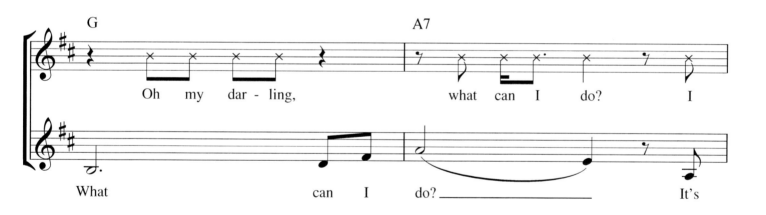

Oh my dar - ling, what can I do? I

What can I do? ___ It's

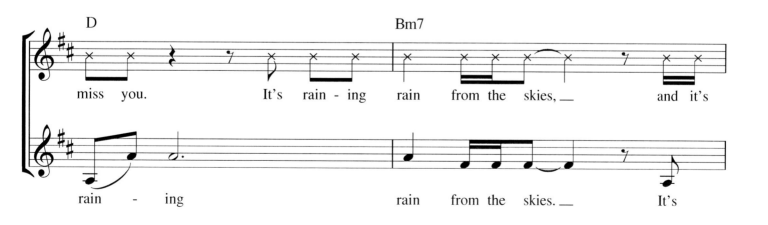

miss you. It's rain - ing rain from the skies, ___ and it's

rain - ing rain from the skies. ___ It's

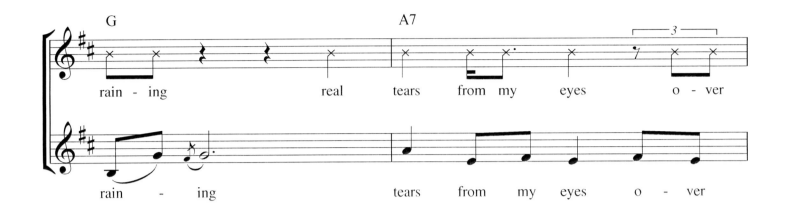

rain - ing   real tears from my eyes   o - ver

rain - ing   tears from my eyes o - ver

you.   Oh,   dear God, make him feel the same way I do right now. ___

you. ___   3. It's rain ___ ing   on

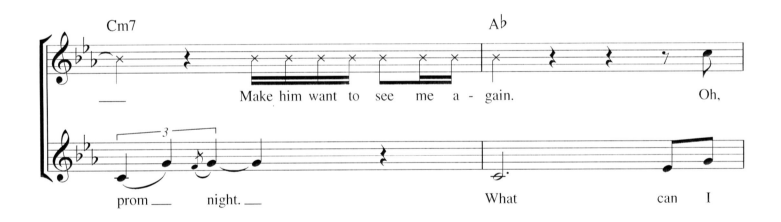

___   Make him want to see me a - gain.   Oh,

prom ___ night. ___   What can I

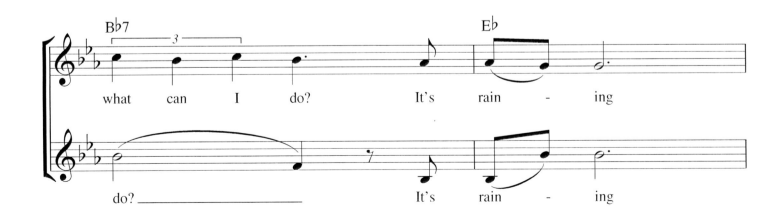

what can I do?   It's rain - ing

do? _____   It's rain - ing

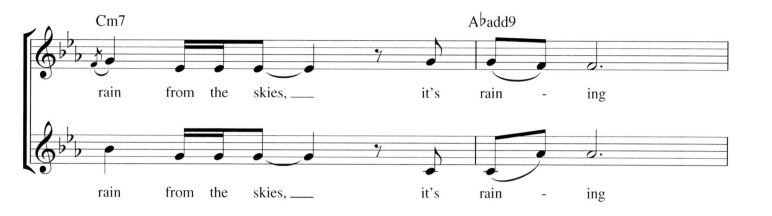

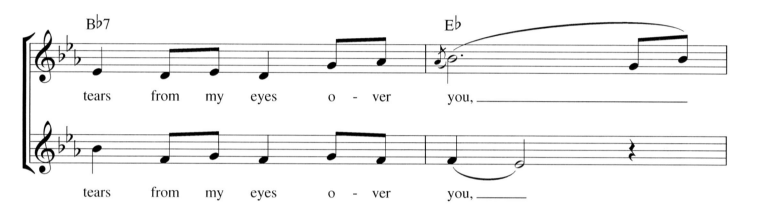

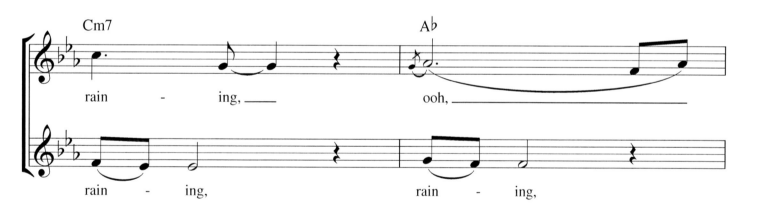

Look at Me, I'm Sandra Dee

Lyric and Music by Warren Casey and Jim Jacobs

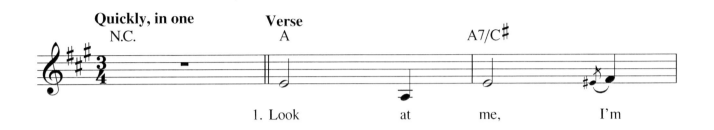

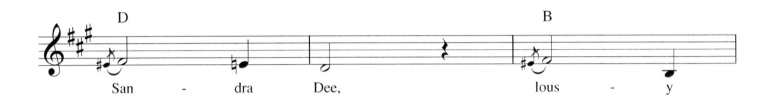

off my silk - y drawers.

Would you pull that crap with An - nette?

Verse

3. As for you, Troy Don - a -

hue, *(Spoken:)* I know _____ what you ____

____ wan - na do. ____ You've got your

crust, I'm no ob - ject of lust, I'm

just plain San - dra Dee.

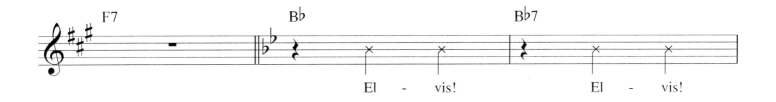

F7   B♭   B♭7

El - vis!   El - vis!

E♭   C7

Let me be! _____   Keep that

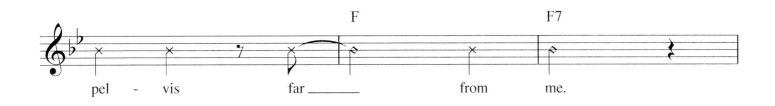

F   F7

pel - vis far _____ from me.

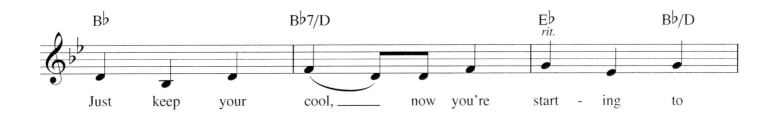

B♭   B♭7/D   E♭   B♭/D
                                                       rit.

Just keep your cool, _____ now you're start - ing to

Freely

C7   N.C.   B♭/F   N.C.   F7   N.C.

drool.   Hey!   Fon - gool!   I'm San - dra Dee.

A tempo

B♭   E♭maj7   E♭6   N.C.   *Repeat and Fade*

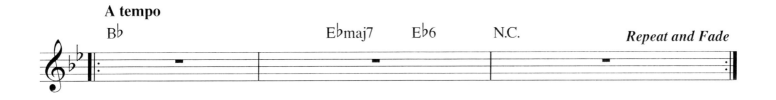

Summer Nights

Lyric and Music by Warren Casey and Jim Jacobs

drift - in' a - way ___ to ___ ah, ah, the sum - mer nights. __

drift - in' a - way ___ to ___ ah, ah, the sum - mer nights. __

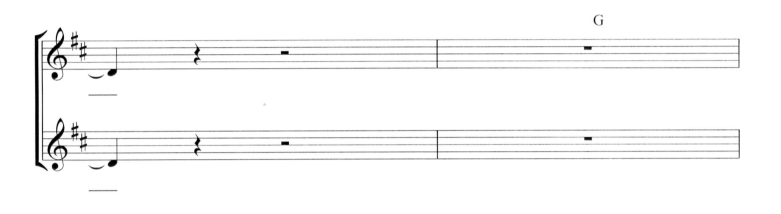

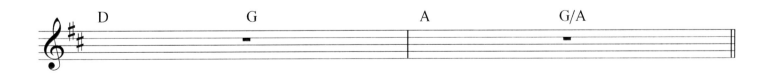

Verse

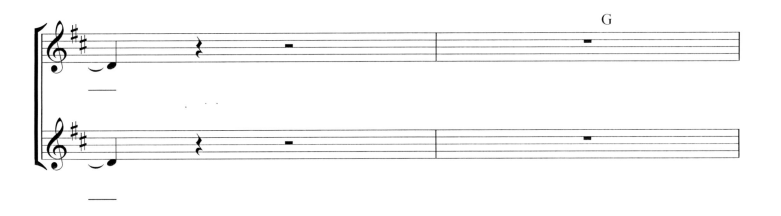

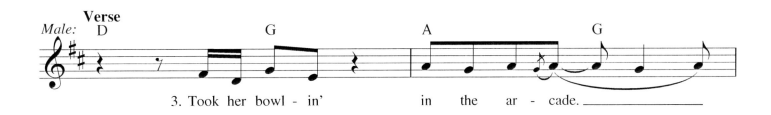

Verse

Male:

3. Took her bowl - in' in the ar - cade.

Female:

We went stroll - in', drank ___ lem - on - ade.

Male: We made out under the dock. _____

Female: We stayed out 'til ten o' - clock. __

Female: Sum - mer fling, don't ___ mean a thing, ___ but ___

Male: Sum - mer fling, don't ___ mean a thing, ___ but

oh, oh, the sum - mer nights. __

oh, oh, the sum - mer nights. __

Verse

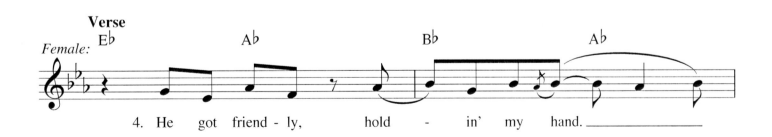

4. He got friend - ly, hold - in' my hand. _____

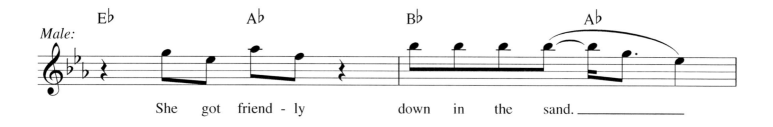

Male:

She got friend - ly down in the sand. _____

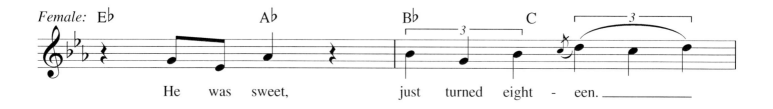

Female:

He was sweet, just turned eight - een. _____

Male:

She was good, you know what I mean. ___

Female:

Sum - mer heat, boy ____ and girl meet, __ but __

Male:

Sum - mer heat, boy ____ and girl meet, __ but

oh, oh, the sum - mer nights. ____

oh, oh, the sum - mer nights. ____

Verse
Slower

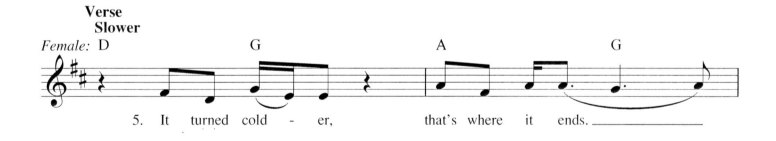

5. It turned cold - er, that's where it ends. _____

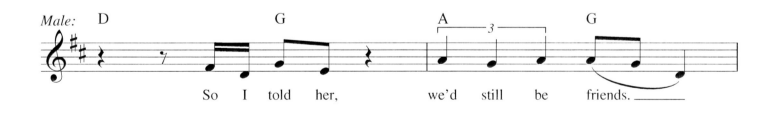

So I told her, we'd still be friends. _____

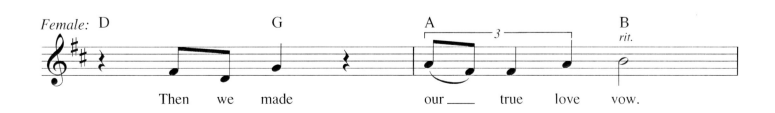

Then we made our ___ true love vow.

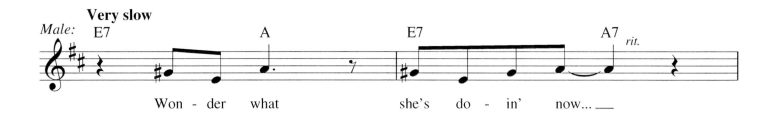

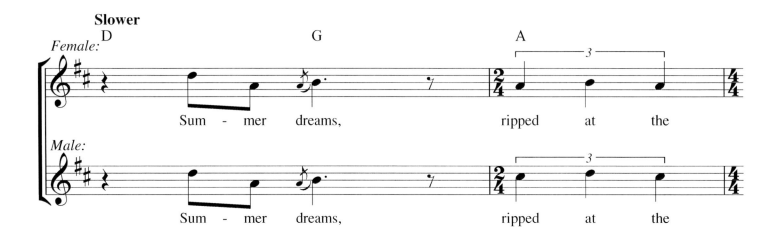

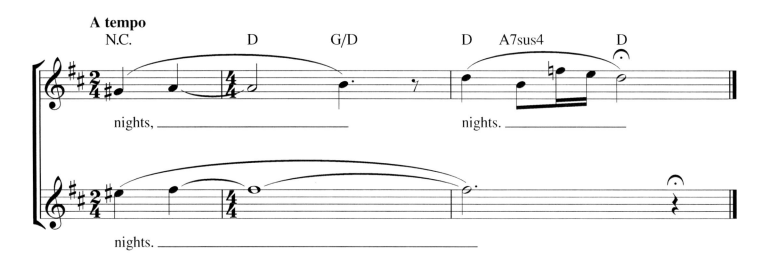

There Are Worse Things I Could Do

Lyric and Music by Warren Casey and Jim Jacobs

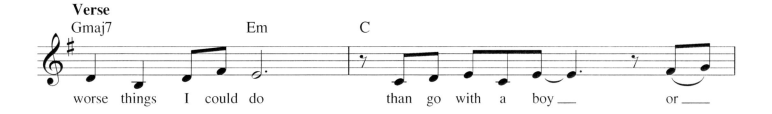

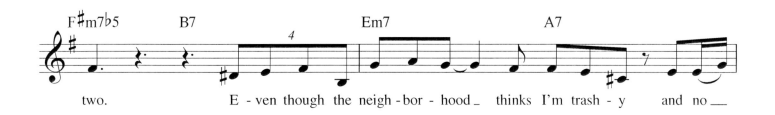

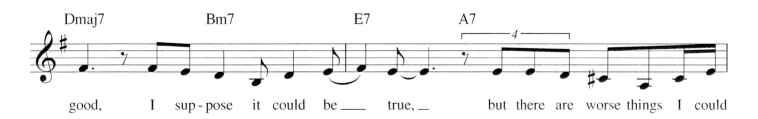

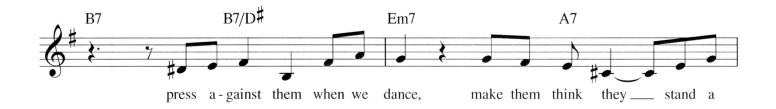

press a-gainst them when we dance, make them think they ___ stand a

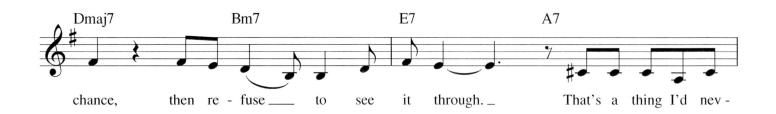

chance, then re-fuse ___ to see it through. _ That's a thing I'd nev -

Bridge

er do. I could stay home ___ ev-'ry night, _

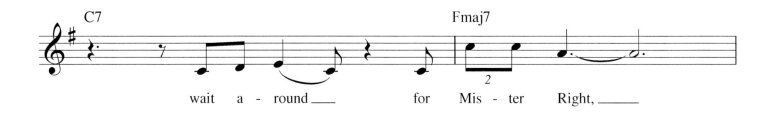

wait a-round ___ for Mis-ter Right, _____

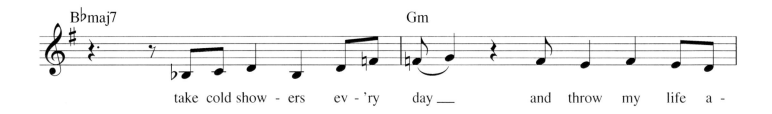

take cold show-ers ev-'ry day ___ and throw my life a -

way on a dream that won't come true.

Verse

3. I could hurt some-one like me _____

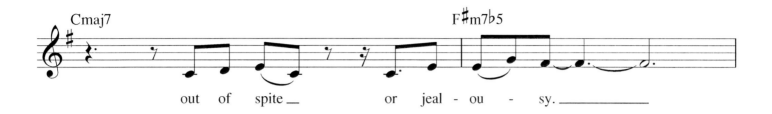

out of spite __ or jeal - ou - sy. _____

I don't steal __ and I don't lie, ____ but I can feel __ and I can

cry, a fact I bet you nev - er _____ knew, _____

____ but to cry _____ in front of you, _____

Freely

that's the worst __ thing __ I could _____ do. _____

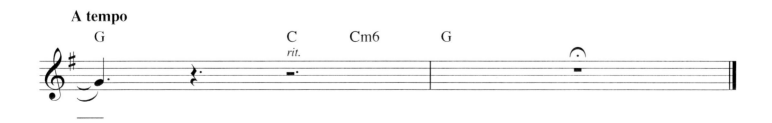

A tempo

__

You're the One That I Want

Words and Music by John Farrar

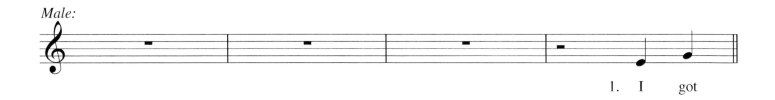

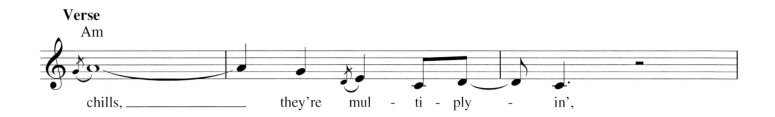

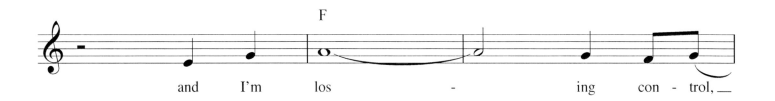

- in'!

Female:

You bet - ter shape up,   'cause __ I

need a man, _____ and my heart __

_____ is set on you. _____ You bet - ter shape

up. ____ You bet - ter un - der - stand, _____

____ to my heart _____ I must be true. __

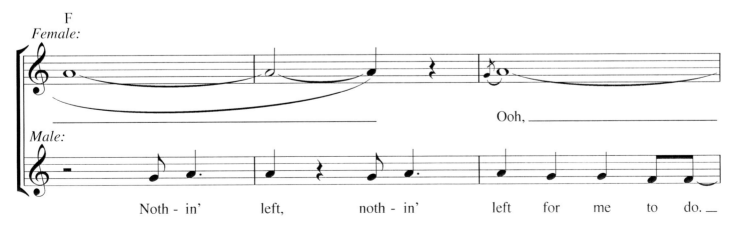

Female:

_____ Ooh, _____

Male:

Noth - in' left, noth - in' left for me to do. __

Chorus

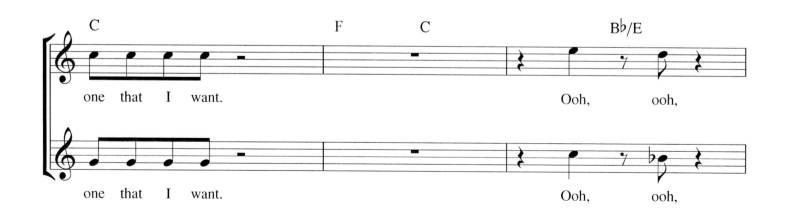

ooh,　　come on　to　me, _____　　　　　　oh yes, in -

ooh,　　come on　to　me, _____　　　　　　oh yes, in -

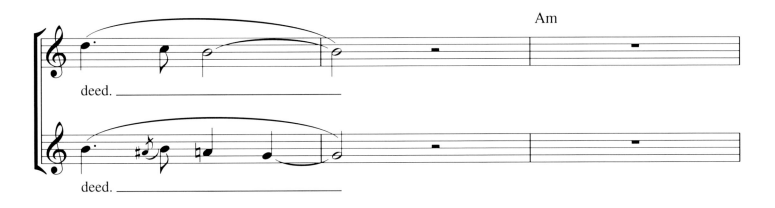

Am

deed. _____

deed. _____

Female:

2. If　　you're　filled _

Verse

Am

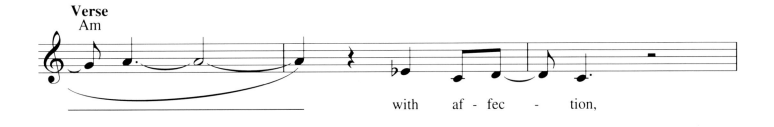

_____　　with　af - fec - tion,

F

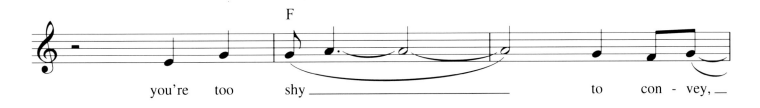

you're　too　shy _____　to　con - vey, __

C

E

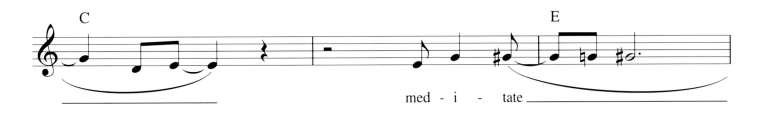

_____　　med - i - tate _____

in my di - rec - tion.

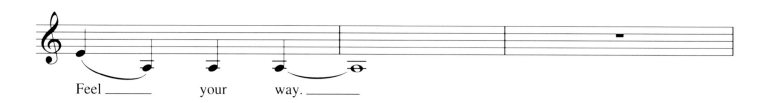

Feel _____ your way. _____

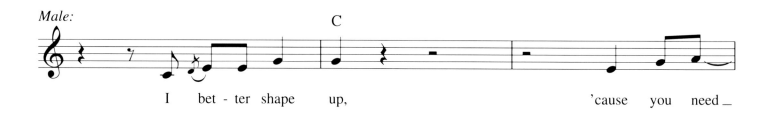

Male:

I bet - ter shape up, 'cause you need _

Female:

I need a man _____ who can keep _

Male:

_____ a man. _____

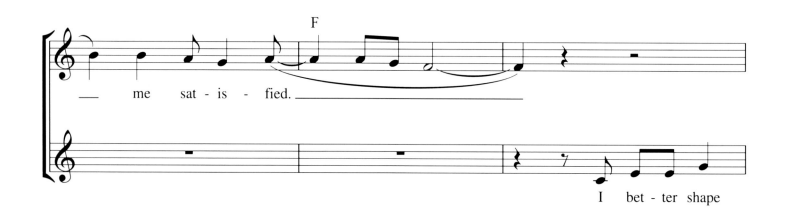

_____ me sat - is - fied. _____

I bet - ter shape

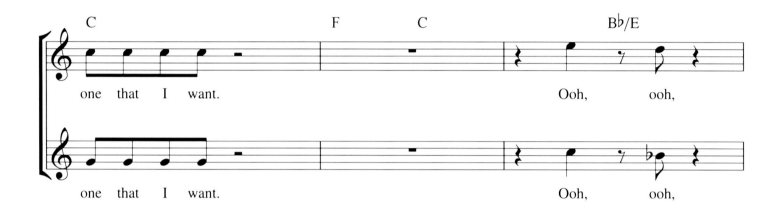

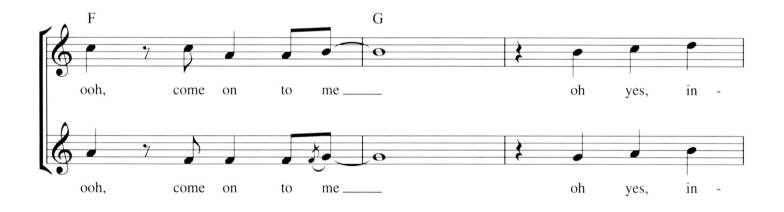

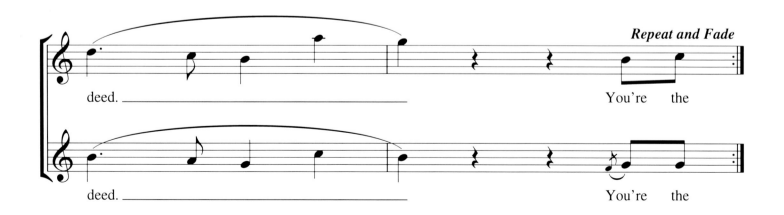